PREDATOR VS. PREY

Lion vs. Gazelle

Mary Meinking

Raintree

Chicago Illinois

www.heinemannraintree.com
Visit our website to find out
more information about
Heinemann-Raintree books.

To order:
☎ Phone 888-454-2279
💻 Visit www.heinemannraintree.com
to browse our catalog and order online.

Edited by Rebecca Rissman, Dan Nunn,
    and Catherine Veitch
Designed by Joanna Hinton Malivoire
Levelling by Jeanne Clidas
Picture research by Hannah Taylor
Production by Victoria Fitzgerald
Originated by Capstone Global Library
Printed and bound in China by CTPS

14 13 12 11 10
10 9 8 7 6 5 4 3 2 1

**Library of Congress Cataloging-in-Publication
Data**
Meinking, Mary.
    Lion vs. gazelle / Mary Meinking.
      p. cm.—(Predator vs. prey)
    Includes bibliographical references and index.
    ISBN 978-1-4109-3934-0 (hc)
    ISBN 978-1-4109-3943-2 (pb)
1. Lion—Food—Juvenile literature. 2. Thomson's gazelle—
Defenses—Juvenile literature. 3. Predation (Biology)—
Juvenile literature. I. Title.
    QL737.C23M45 2011
    599.757'153—dc22
    2010016914

Acknowledgments
We would like to thank the following for permission
to reproduce photographs: Alamy Images pp. 20 (©
Gary Dublanko), 21 (© Philip Dalton), 22 (© Steve Bloom
Images), 27 (© Bill Gozansky); ardea.com p. 18 (©
Ferrero-Labat); FLPA pp. 8 (Jurgen & Christine Sohns), 10
(Martin B Withers), 14 (Minden Pictures/Mitsuaki Iwago),
23 (Michael Gore), 25 (Ariadne Van Zandbergen), 29
(Malcolm Schuyl); Getty Images p. 9 (Joseph Van Os);
istockphoto pp. 6 (© Carl Fourie), 11 (© brytta), 24 (©
Britta Kasholm-Tengve), 26 (© Peter Malsbury); naturepl
pp. 13 (Francois Savigny), 15 (Peter Blackwell), 16 (Tony
Heald); Photolibrary pp. 4 (Peter Arnold Images/ Martin
Harvey), 5 (Oxford Scientific/ David W Breed), 7 (age
fotostock/ Werner Bollmann), 12 (Birgit Koch), 17 (Fritz
Poelking), 28 (Oxford Scientific/ Elliott Neep); Science
Photo Library p. 19 (William Ervin).

Cover photographs of an African lion reproduced with
permission of Photolibrary (Oxford Scientific/ David
W Breed), and a Thompson's gazelle reproduced with
permission of Alamy Images (© Balman Photography).

We would like to thank Michael Bright for his invaluable
help in the preparation of this book.

Every effort has been made to contact copyright holders
of any material reproduced in this book. Any omissions
will be rectified in subsequent printings if notice is given
to the publisher.

Some words are shown in bold, **like this**. You can find
out what they mean by looking in the glossary.

Contents

Claws vs. Horns

Claws rip! Horns stab! Two animals meet on a dry **plains** battleground! Here is the frightening beast, the lion. It's up against a bouncing challenger, the gazelle.

gazelle

4

lion

5

These **competitors** live in Africa's **grasslands**. Both have strengths that will help them in this battle.

PREDATOR
African **lioness**

LENGTH: 10 feet

WEIGHT: 300 pounds

HEIGHT: 3 feet

Key

where African lions and Thomson's gazelles live

PREY
Thomson's gazelle

LENGTH: 3 feet

WEIGHT: 60 pounds

HEIGHT: 2 feet

Africa

Girl Power

Around 10 to 30 lions live in a group called a **pride**. Most are **lionesses** from the same family. When the lionesses hunt together, they catch more **prey**.

mane

Did You Know?
There are usually one or two male lions in each pride. They do not hunt with the group. Their big **manes** would give them away if they tried to hide!

9

Super Senses

The gazelle has great **vision**. But when it is in tall grass it cannot see its enemies. It uses its excellent senses of smell and hearing instead. Staying in a **herd** means there are more noses and ears to smell and hear **prey**!

Did You Know?
The gazelle is a tan color. This helps it blend in with the dry grass.

Who's Hungry?

Lions are **carnivores**, or animals that eat meat. There are many mouths to feed in each **pride**. So the **lionesses** need to hunt and kill enough meat for everyone.

Did You know?
Most lions eat 15 pounds of meat a day! That's like eating 60 hamburgers every day!

Stalking Game

From a hilltop, four **lionesses** watch a **herd** of gazelles. They're looking for a young, old, or hurt gazelle. They are easier to catch.

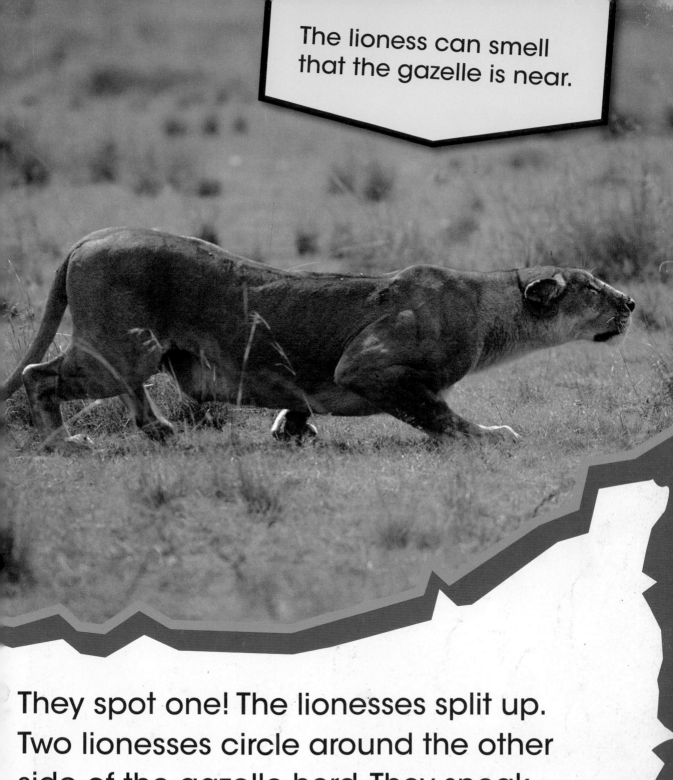

The lioness can smell that the gazelle is near.

They spot one! The lionesses split up. Two lionesses circle around the other side of the gazelle herd. They sneak toward the **prey**.

They creep closer. The plan is for one **lioness** to scare the gazelle toward the other two. When the lioness is near the gazelle, she charges at it.

Did You Know?

Lions have soft pads on the bottom of their feet. These pads help them **stalk prey** quietly. It is like wearing running shoes.

17

A gazelle sees the **lioness** coming. It **stots**, or jumps straight up. This tells the lioness the gazelle is too healthy to catch. The stotting also tells the other gazelles that danger is nearby. The gazelles run in every direction.

Did You Know?

A gazelle can jump up to 10 feet high. That's as high as four school desks on top of each other.

The **lioness** runs after the closest gazelle. The gazelle starts running. The lioness's thick muscular legs pound the dry ground trying to catch it. It keeps low so the gazelle cannot see it.

The **lioness** cannot run far. She needs to catch the gazelle soon. She chases it at 36 miles per hour. That is faster than a car goes in a town!

23

The gazelle runs in a **zigzag,** or Z-shaped pattern. It's trying to lose the **lioness**. The lioness stays with the gazelle for several minutes. But soon the gazelle goes one way when the lioness goes the other. The lioness loses the gazelle in the tall grass.

Did You Know?
Lions do not always catch their food. Often they will steal **prey** from other animals.

And the Winner Is...

...the gazelle! The gazelle is not big enough to fight off enemies. So its best defence is to run! Its speed and being able to turn quickly saved it from being the **lioness's** next meal.

What Are the Odds?

Because **lionesses** are slow, they rely on teamwork. What one lioness misses, another can catch. So lions make great team players!

Did You Know?

A lioness hunting alone only catches **prey** once every seven tries. But when she hunts with others, they catch prey every three tries.

Glossary

carnivore animal that eats meat

grasslands land where mostly grasses grow

herd group of animals living together

lioness female lion

mane long fur that grows around the head of male lions

plain flat land with few trees

predator animal that hunts other animals

prey animal that is hunted by other animals for food

pride group of lions, usually one or two males and several females with their cubs

stalk sneak up on prey

stotting jumping high with stiff legs

vision eyesight

zigzag several sharp turns to change direction

Find Out More

Books

Encyclopedia of *Animals.* New York: Dorling Kindersley, 2006.

Spilsbury, Louise and Richard. *Watching Lions in Africa.* Chicago: Heinemann Library, 2007.

Turner, Pamela. *A Life in the Wild: George Schaller's Struggle to Save the Last Great Beasts.* New York: Farrar, Straus, and Giroux, 2008.

Websites

http://animals.nationalgeographic.com/animals/mammals/gazelle/
Find out more about Thomson's gazelles on this Website.

http://kids.nationalgeographic.com/kids/animals/creaturefeature/lion
On this Website you can learn about lions, watch videos, and print off collector's cards.

http://www.bbc.co.uk/bigcat/
Visit the Big Cat Website to watch videos and find out about prides of lions living in Africa.

Index